The HERO BOOK

Learning Lessons from the People You Admire

I0892076

by Ellen Sabin

and ______________________________

WRITE YOUR NAME HERE

WATERING CAN® PRESS

WATERING CAN®

Growing Kids with Character

When you care about things and nurture them, they will grow healthy, strong, and happy and, in turn, will make the world a better place.

Several website addresses (URLs) are provided in this book as resource references. The publisher does not maintain these sites, all of which were active and valid at the time of publication. Please note that over time, URLs and/or their content may change. We regret any inconvenience this may cause readers.

Written by Ellen Sabin
Illustrated by Kerren Barbas
Designed by Heather Zschock

ISBN # 0-9759868-1-3
Printed in Hong Kong

Website address: www.wateringcanpress.com

Dear ______________________________,

Because you are such a nice, wonderful, kind, and caring person, I am giving you this **HERO BOOK**.

We all have heroes—special people we know or have heard about who we admire and look up to.

Heroes come in all different types, sizes, colors, and ages. Once you start thinking about the qualities that you like in people, you'll see that there are special people all around!

THE HERO BOOK is an activity book, a diary, and a scrapbook that lets you think about the things that you admire in others.

You'll also see that you have tons of qualities that make **YOU** a hero too!

From, ______________________________

Since this is about heroes, here are some "thank-yous" to some of mine:

To my Nanny, for her love ❤
I am truly blessed to have had a grandmother who is my hero.

To my parents, sisters, and Sarah, Lorna, Anne, and Julie—
who each possess unique and incredible qualities that I admire and strive to emulate.

To all the folks who do everyday acts
that inspire others to be their best.

A NOTE TO PARENTS

Our mission: To make the world more beautiful—one child at a time.

We know that once children think about the **qualities and characteristics** that they admire,
they will view the people who they meet or hear about through the lens of those qualities;
they will seek to emulate those qualities and characteristics;
they will find role models who inspire them to be their best; and
they will, in turn, grow to be their best.

We hope this book inspires them.

Perhaps it will also create a keepsake, showing their values, ideals,
and aspirations of ways of being and acting. This activity book will become
a scrapbook of their journey into finding role models for their own behavior.

Table of Contents

What is The HERO BOOK?

Welcome to Your **HERO BOOK!**

A **HERO** is someone you admire.

Think about what makes your heroes so special to you.

- Maybe you like how they act or things that they do or say.
- Maybe you like them because they are smart, talented, or caring toward others.

The things you admire are called **QUALITIES**.

In this book, you get to think about why you admire people and how you can learn from them.

Sometimes, heroes can become your role models. That's when you want to be more like them and have some of their qualities.

This book will help you do just that!

So what are you waiting for?
Turn the page and get started!

How does THE HERO BOOK work?

There are many different kinds of HEROES.

YOU get to choose YOUR heroes and decide what makes them special to you!

First You think about the things that you admire in people.

Next You think about your heroes and their qualities—how they act or what they do that seems wonderful to you.

Then

You get to look at all the great qualities that you have—the ones that make YOU a hero!

Next

You think of things that you can do to have the qualities that you admire in your heroes—you act in all the ways that you admire in them so that you can be the best person you can be.

REMEMBER: This is YOUR book. Along the way, you can keep a journal, draw pictures, take notes, and collect ideas about all the things that you admire about yourself and your heroes.

What Is A HERO?

A Hero Is Someone You Admire,

someone you look up to,
someone you can learn from,
someone who has qualities you would like to have.

There are many different reasons to admire someone. And there are all kinds of different people who you will meet or learn about in your life who can be your heroes or role models.

- Heroes can be people you like because they are hard-working and have accomplished something great. These might be people you know or maybe someone that you learned about in school, in a book, or on television.

- They can be people you think are really smart and have great ideas.

- Maybe they are people who are really good at something, like sports or music, and you admire them for their skills and talents.

- They can be people you like because they are brave and do courageous things to help others.

- They can be people you think are very nice and do things that are loving and caring. You might admire them because they always make you or other people feel good.

Your **HEROES** can be anyone who you think is special or does special things. They can be your role models and inspire you. They can teach you lessons and help you become even more special.

Well-Known Heroes

Sometimes a hero is someone you know.
Heroes can also be people who you have never met.

HEROES can be well-known people from history who you learn about in school or from reading books. Maybe they did things a long time ago that you think are great!

HEROES can be people you see on television or hear about who are doing things nearby or far away.

Can you think of some well-known people who you admire or look up to?

Write about them on the next page

YOUR Well-Known Heroes

Person:

What do you admire about this person?

Person:

What do you admire about this person?

Person:

What do you admire about this person?

Person:

What do you admire about this person?

Everyday Heroes

Not all heroes are famous.

Many of your heroes might be people you know from your neighborhood, school, church/temple, or community.

Heroes can be people you see every day like your parents, teachers, or friends.

These people can be your heroes for the things that you see them do, how they act, or how they make your life special.

Who are some of your everyday heroes?

You know what to do now

YOUR Everyday Heroes

Person:

What do you admire about this person?

Person:

What do you admire about this person?

Person:

What do you admire about this person?

Person:

What do you admire about this person?

What Are the QUALITIES of Your Heroes?

Circle the Words

You've already written about what you admire in your well-known and everyday heroes. The things you admire are their qualities. Sometimes it is really easy to see these qualities in your heroes. Other times, you have to look closer to find all the qualities you admire in people.

Can you find all of the qualities listed below in the puzzle? Make sure you look up, down, and across. Circle the words when you find them.

B	R	A	V	E	L	H	L	G
D	G	T	Y	D	E	O	N	I
E	S	H	A	R	I	N	G	V
T	A	L	E	N	T	E	D	I
A	P	E	E	I	Q	S	C	N
J	U	T	M	X	K	T	B	G
F	A	I	R	O	I	G	O	S
D	F	C	E	Q	N	U	I	D
C	O	N	F	I	D	E	N	T

WORDS:

- ATHLETIC
- BRAVE
- CONFIDENT
- FAIR
- GIVING
- HONEST
- KIND
- SHARING
- TALENTED

Maybe **COURAGE** is something you admire in people.

People show courage in many different ways.

If someone is afraid to try something new and then does it anyway, that's courage.

Maybe you, a friend, or a classmate stood up for someone who was bullied or picked on. That's courage, too.

Here are two stories about courage that you can help finish! Read each one and then complete the story by writing how the character can show courage.

Sue is very, very shy in school. Every time the teacher asks her questions, she gets embarrassed and turns red. One day, the teacher asks if anyone knows the answer to a math question. Sue knows the answer. How can she be brave and show courage?

....

....

Walter is visiting his aunt when she gets very ill and can't get out of her chair. How can Walter be brave in this situation?

....

....

Heroes for Their **COURAGE**

This fireman just ran in the house to help save the people and put out the fire.
He was very brave!

Can you think of someone you know who did something brave and showed courage?
Write about it here:

Maybe **FAIRNESS** and **HONESTY** are things you admire in people.

Every day, people make choices about how to act and what to do.
You may admire people when they do the "right thing" and are fair and honest.

- MAYBE you look up to people who stand up for what they believe.
- MAYBE you respect people who help those who are treated unfairly.

Ask someone in your family or your teacher to tell you about someone in history who THEY admire and think was a hero for being fair and honest.

Write about that person here:

Heroes for Their **FAIRNESS** and **HONESTY**

This woman makes big decisions for many people. Sometimes what she says isn't very popular, but she is honest and fair to help make sure that people are treated well in the world.

Think of someone who is always fair and honest. Who is this person and why do you admire him or her?

Maybe you admire people with **BIG HEARTS** who show LOVE and CARE.

People with big hearts show love and care every day to others and make them feel special and happy in lots of ways.

Make a list of people who you think have really big hearts!

Heroes for Their **BIG HEARTS**

Every day, these parents give love and care to their child. They make him feel safe and loved, and always do nice things to make sure he grows up strong, healthy, and happy.

Tell a story about someone who gives you love every day. What does this person do, and how does it make you feel?

Maybe you admire people who are charitable and do things to **HELP OTHER PEOPLE.**

People who are charitable use their time, energy, or money to help others. They are concerned about other people and they take actions to help them.

People help others all the time. They do big things and small things. They do things for people who they know or even for strangers they've never met.

They care about things—like helping people who are sick or hungry or cleaning up litter or making the world more peaceful.

Here's a list of some things that people do when they want to help others:

- Share their lunch
- Donate used toys
- Help a friend with homework
- Cook food to bring to someone who is hungry
- Clean the house
- Bring clothes to a place to give to people who are cold

Heroes for HELPING OTHERS

These people are helping to build a house for a family that doesn't have a home. They are giving their time, energy, and care to help other people who don't have some of the things that they have.

Can you think of other ways that people are charitable? Write about it here.

Maybe you admire people who **WORK HARD** and **FOCUS** to become excellent at their skills.

Think about what makes people good at their skills or talents.

Whether they are terrific at basketball, ballet, piano, or chess—whether they are famous on TV or the best in your house—people admired for their talents all share things in common!

Fill in the blanks below and see what all these heroes do:

They s__udy hard.

They __ractice a lot!

They try and try and t__ __ some more!

Heroes for Their **HARD WORK** and **FOCUS**

This man is one of the best runners ever. He practices every day so that he can be faster and faster. He concentrates, learns everything he can about his sport, and has a lot of discipline.

Can you think of someone who is very talented and skilled? What do you admire about this person?

Maybe you admire people who **BELIEVE IN THEMSELVES** and in their **IDEAS.**

There are so many great ideas and inventions in our world. It takes more than just creativity or being smart to make an idea work.

When people come up with new ideas, they have to have confidence in themselves to say, "I CAN DO IT!"

Sometimes they have to try many, many times before their idea works. Sometimes people make fun of them or tell them it will never work—BUT THEY JUST KEEP ON TRYING!

Someone made the first telephone, the first tunnel, and the first lightbulb. Someone figured out that the world is round and not flat, and someone had the idea to fly to the moon!

Someone had an idea to write your favorite book. Someone decided to put together all the ingredients to make your favorite food. Someone invented the toys and games you love most.

All these people believed in themselves and in their ideas!

Heroes for Their **CONFIDENCE** and **IDEAS**

These people invented something completely new. Before they worked on their projects, no one knew how to make an airplane fly or how to build a bridge.

Can you think of some inventions that are really great? List them below and then see if you can learn about the person who invented them!

Maybe you admire people who do **KIND**, **NICE**, and **THOUGHTFUL** things all the time.

Here's an "Everyday Hero" rhyme about people who are kind!

Doctors and nurses
Take care of people every day.
They are wonderfully giving
In their work and their ways.

Coaches and teammates
Can be folks you think are great.
When they cheer you on or teach you
For their kindness—they're first-rate!

Your grandpa or neighbor
Or babysitter who show they care
When they read you a story
And take time to share.

Teachers are wonderful
And they may get your celebration
As high on your list
For their everyday dedication.

Your friends and your family
Do things all the time
That you admire and can think about
As you finish this "everyday hero" rhyme!

Heroes for Their ACTS OF KINDNESS

This boy is including the new kid in school in his group of friends. He knows that it is nice to make people feel welcomed.

Who do you admire for their kindness? Below, write a "hero rhyme" about this person and the nice things they do.

Your Turn!

There are so many qualities that you may find special in people.
You've thought about some of them in this chapter.

Now it's your turn! Can you think of another quality that you think is great?

Maybe you admire people who are ______________________________ .
Now, draw a picture below of someone who shows this quality.

Circle the Words

Find the words on this page that describe things that you admire about people or ways they act that you think are great.

generous
messy
kind
sharing
athletic
MEAN
smart
dishonest
GREEDY
TRUSTING
hard-working
GIVING
creative
selfish
FAIR
brave
irresponsible
funny
confident
unkind
LAZY
SPIRITUAL

What are some other words that describe the qualities that you admire in people?

1. ....

2. ....

3. ....

4. ....

5. ....

6. ....

7. ....

8. ....

9. ....

10. ....

Who Are YOUR Heroes?

Your Heroes

Now that you've thought about the qualities that you admire, it's time to think about even more heroes who have those qualities!

You've already written about some of your heroes, but can you think of other people you look up to and admire?

Think about the different qualities we have discussed:

- courage
- fairness
- honesty
- caring
- charity
- creativity
- confidence
- talent

Think about the other qualities you came up with on your own.

Now, turn the page and write about some of YOUR heroes

Your Heroes

Write down more of your heroes below. Make sure to include what you admire about them. Don't forget that you can include well-known and everyday heroes.

Person:

____

What do you admire about this person?

____

____

____

Person:

____

What do you admire about this person?

____

____

____

Person:

____

What do you admire about this person?

____

____

____

Draw an Everyday HERO

Draw a picture of someone in your family who you admire.

What do you admire about this person?

Write a Letter!

Write a letter to one of your heroes—it can be to a well-known hero or to one of your everyday heroes.

After all, it is always nice for us to thank our heroes and the people who are special to us.

In your letter, you can tell your hero all about why you like and admire him or her.

Then, copy this letter onto a piece of paper. If the hero is someone you know, you can send the letter in the mail, or give it to him or her the next time you see them. If you want to write a letter to a well-known hero, maybe a parent or another adult can help you find an address where you can mail it.

Your Hero Letter!

#1

Dear ______________________,

From, ______________________

Write Your Own HERO Story!

There are many fictional stories about heroes who have saved the day or helped people in need. Can you make up a story about a hero?

Start by answering the questions below.

Who is the main character of your story?

What hero qualities does your character have?

Where does your story take place?

Now make up a story about your hero. We even left room for you to draw a picture! Then share the story and picture with your friends and family.

Your Hero Story Here

My Hero

YOU Are A Hero!

Hey! Don't forget!
YOU are a hero, too!

You've spent a lot of time thinking about what you admire in other people and choosing your heroes.

There are also MANY great things about you, too!

You have some of the same qualities that you admire in your heroes.

Maybe there are even ways that you can make yourself and your life even better by learning lessons from your heroes.

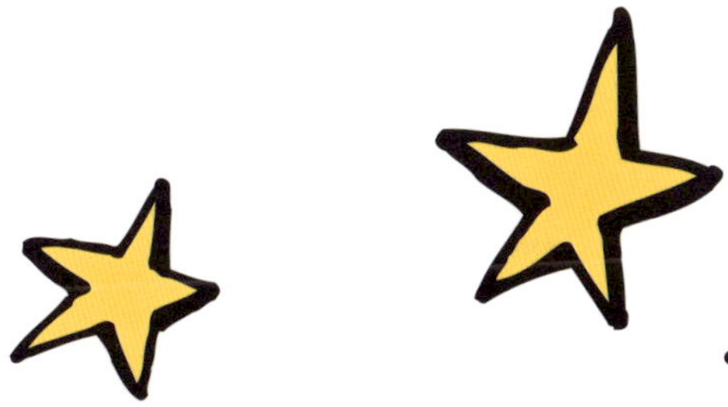

HERO Poem

Your heroes might show courage
And be very strong and brave,
Like soldiers and firemen
For all the lives they save.

Your heroes might like to be fair
And believe things should be right,
Like politicians who make laws,
Or teachers who say "don't fight."

Your heroes might be talented
At music, sports, or art,
Like famous people on TV,
Or a classmate who is smart.

Your heroes might help people
And show love to those they meet,
Like doctors who make people better,
Or friends who are so sweet.

Your heroes can be anyone
If you admire what they do.
And always remember this one thing—
YOU can be a HERO, too!

Fill in the Blanks

I am very proud of myself when I ______________________________

____

____

I work hard to be good at ______________________________

This is what I do to try to get even better at it: ____________________

____

____

____

____

I did something that was just like ____________________ would do.

This is what I did: ______________________________

____

____

____

____

Your Hero Story

Write a story about something you did that made YOU a HERO to someone else!

Your Hero Qualities

You probably have some of the same qualities as your heroes!
Think about ways you are like your heroes and list them in the boxes below.

I am:

What Do You Learn from Your HEROES?

One of the best ways to show what you admire about someone is to try to be like them in the ways that you think are great.

If you admire a hero for their kindness, try to be more kind and loving in that way, too.

What can you do that is kind and loving?

Show your bravery, like your heroes do.

What can you do that will take courage?

Find ways to help others and be charitable—just like your heroes.

Can you think of some ways that you can help other people?

Work hard at your skills so that you can be very talented like your heroes might be.

★ What skill would you like to be better at?

★ What can you do to become better at that skill?

Believe in your ideas and stick with them. Then come up with inventions or things that are new and different.

★ List some projects or inventions that you want to create. They can be anything!

★ What else can you do to be like your heroes?

You are a hero!

EXPRESS Yourself

Your Very Own
HERO JOURNAL and SCRAPBOOK

We're leaving the next couple of pages blank for you.

Here's why: We know we didn't think of everything. You probably have other **GREAT, FUN** ideas about how to use these pages!

You can:

Fill these pages with photos of the people you admire!

Create drawings and pictures showing heroic things YOU have done!

Use these pages to write a hero story or a poem about one of your heroes!

Write another letter to tell one of your heroes what you admire about him or her.

There are so many great ideas for using these pages!

GOOD
CONDUCT

OTHER STUFF

Congratulations!

You've learned all about your heroes and why you admire them. This HERO BOOK certificate shows that you can be someone's hero, too!

THE HERO BOOK

This certificate is awarded to

....

WRITE YOUR NAME HERE

for being a true hero!

....

DATE

Now it's your job to spread the word! Tell your friends and family about the true qualities of a hero and watch them shine, too!

Reference Ideas for Adults

There are many ways to teach children about heroes and heroic qualities.

We found a couple of fun hero-related websites that inspired us, so we thought we'd share them with you.

www.myhero.com

MY HERO is a not-for-profit educational web project that celebrates the best of humanity. Its mission is to enlighten and inspire people of all ages with an ever-growing Internet archive of hero stories from around the world.

www.time.com/time/time100/heroes/

TIME profiles the 20 most influential heroes and icons of the 20th century, including Charles Lindbergh, Muhammad Ali, Anne Frank, and Helen Keller.

www.giraffe.org

A not-for-profit organization that seeks to train tomorrow's heroes and find and commend people with vision and courage who are willing to "stick their necks out" for the common good.

Be a Hero!

We'd love your help to expand THE HERO BOOK

Go to www.wateringcanpress.com to:

- share the ideas or experiences you or a child have had with THE HERO BOOK,
- order additional books for friends/family members or donate copies to an organization of your choice,
- learn about bulk purchases for schools, stores, and organizations,
- view the free HERO BOOK Teacher's Guide, and
- see other Watering Can® series books.

Be a HERO by GIVING to others...

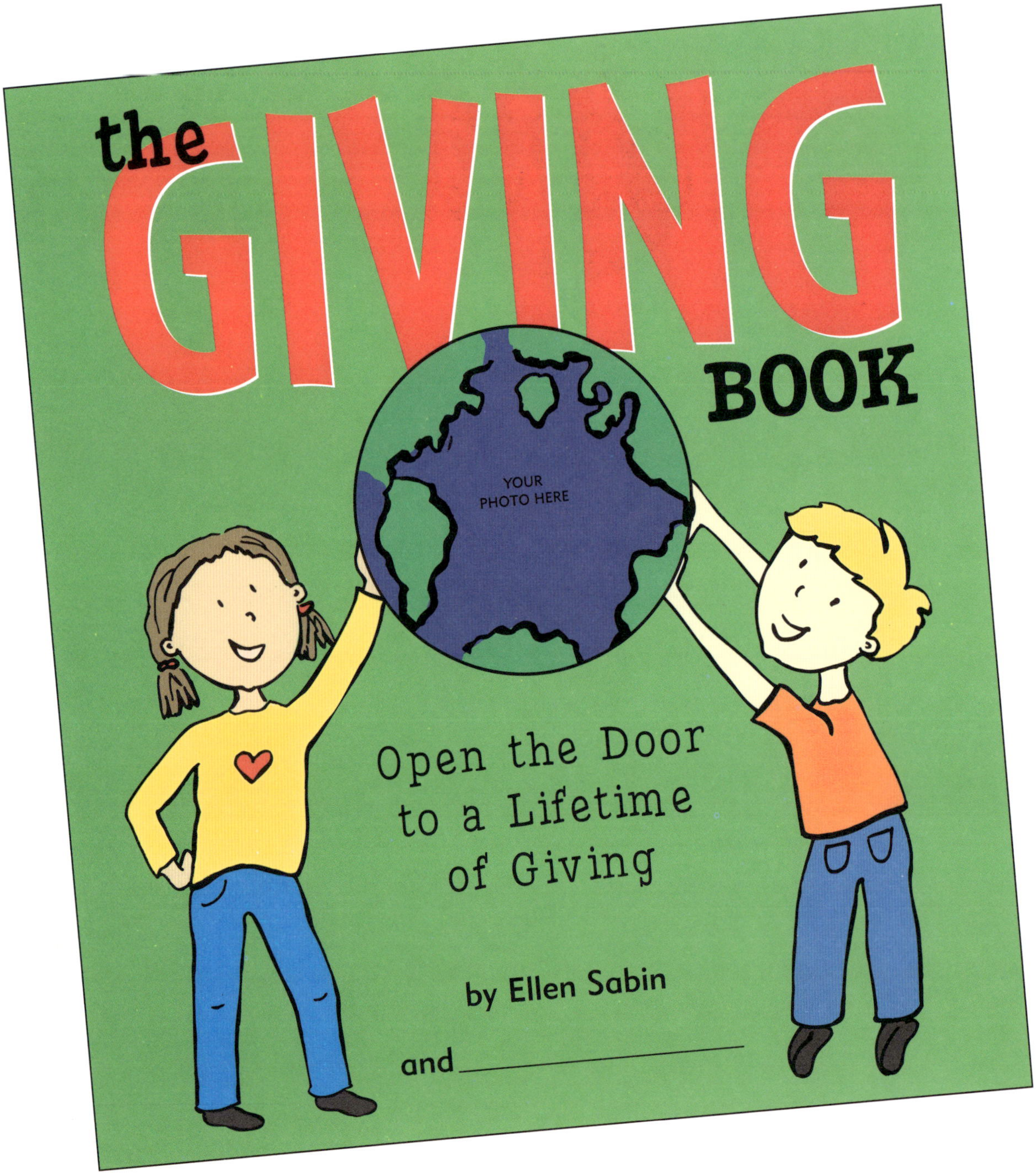

One way you can be a hero is to help other people and make the world around you a better place. Being giving and charitable is SO important and you can do SO much to help others. Want to get started?

THE GIVING BOOK is a really fun way to be a hero for other people. With this book you can:

- Think about your wishes and dreams for making the world a better place!
- Appreciate how you feel when people are kind and giving to you!
- List all the different things you have to share with other people, like your talents, your time, and the things you have!
- Do fun activities with your family or friends to help other people—you can even do things to help animals or the planet!
- Learn ways to save money to give to your favorite charities or organizations!
- Realize how powerful your actions can be and how much of a difference you can make!

You are someone's hero!

We hope that you enjoy
the wonderful **HEROES**
in your life and celebrate
the qualities that make
YOU a hero too!